AF084400

Tidy-Up Time

by Jackie Walter and Noopur Thakur

It is time to tidy up.

We put the water bottles in the box.

We put the books on the shelves.

We tidy up the paper.
We put the scissors
in the box.

We put the lids on the pens.
We put the pens in the pot.

We put the aprons on the pegs.

We tidy up the paints.
We put the brushes in the pots.

We put the lids back on the glue sticks.

The classroom is tidy.

Talk and Explore

Ask your child to describe each picture below, in their own words, pointing to each picture in turn.

Look at the different stages of tidying up and which items are put away in each picture.

Independent Reading

This series is designed to provide an opportunity for your child to read on their own. These notes are written for you to help your child choose a book and to read it independently.
In school, your child's teacher will often be using reading books which have been banded to support the process of learning to read.
Use the book band colour your child is reading in school to help you make a good choice. *Tidy-Up Time* is a good choice for children reading at Yellow Band in their classroom to read independently.
The aim of independent reading is to read this book with ease, so that your child enjoys the story and relates it to their own experiences.

About the book
This information book looks at how a class go about tidying up their classroom at the end of a school day.

Before reading
Help your child to learn how to make good choices by asking: "Why did you choose this book? Why do you think you will enjoy it?" Look at the cover together and ask: "What do you think the book will be about?" Support your child to think of what they already know about the context. Read the title aloud and ask: "What do you think the children will be tidying up? Why do you think that?" Remind your child that they can try to sound out the letters to make a word if they get stuck.
Decide together whether your child will read the story independently or read it aloud to you. When books are short, as at Yellow Band, your child may wish to do both!

During reading
If reading aloud, support your child if they hesitate or ask for help by telling the word. Remind your child of what they know and what they can do independently.
If reading to themselves, remind your child that they can come and ask for your help if stuck.

After reading
Support understanding of the book by asking your child to tell you what they found out. Did they learn anything new? Did anything surprise them?
As you discuss the book, you might begin to use vocabulary such close, stack, pile, clean, shut and finish.
Give your child a chance to respond to the book: "Can you think of other things that you might tidy up at school or at home?"
Use the Talk and Explore activity to encourage your child to talk about what they have learned.

Extending learning
Talk about the importance of putting things away and keeping things clean. Ask "what would happen if no one tidied up?" Think about other times of the day that it is important to follow a routine and to tidy up, for example after a meal or after playing with toys. Create a list of things that are tidied up in a typical day.

In the classroom, your child's teacher may be introducing punctuation. On a few of the pages, check your child can recognise capital letters and full stops by asking them to point these out.

Franklin Watts
First published in Great Britain in 2021
by The Watts Publishing Group

Copyright © The Watts Publishing Group 2021

All rights reserved.

Series Editors: Jackie Hamley and Melanie Palmer
Development Editors and Series Advisors: Dr Sue Bodman and Glen Franklin
Series Designers: Cathryn Gilbert and Peter Scoulding

A CIP catalogue record for this book is
available from the British Library.

ISBN 978 1 4451 7683 3 (hbk)
ISBN 978 1 4451 7681 9 (pbk)
ISBN 978 1 4451 7682 6 (library ebook)
ISBN 978 1 4451 8340 4 (ebook)

Printed in China

Franklin Watts
An imprint of
Hachette Children's Group
Part of The Watts Publishing Group
Carmelite House
50 Victoria Embankment
London EC4Y 0DZ

An Hachette UK Company
www.hachette.co.uk

www.franklinwatts.co.uk